CHESS

T0008860

KINGFISHER

LONDON & NEW YORK

KINGFISHER
LONDON & NEW YORK

Text and design copyright © Toucan Books Ltd. 2022
Illustrations copyright © Simon Basher 2022
www.basherscience.com

First published 2022 in the United States by Kingfisher
120 Broadway, New York, NY 10271
Kingfisher is an imprint of Macmillan Children's Books, London
All rights reserved.

Author: Tom Jackson
Consultant: Rich Dampare Smartt, Chess Cubs Ltd.
Editor: Anna Southgate
Designer: Dave Jones
Proofreader: Richard Beatty

With thanks to Sandra Djukic and Adam Bukojemski
for their help with the manuscript and board setups

Dedicated to Nikia

Distributed in the U.S. and Canada by Macmillan,
120 Broadway, New York, NY 10271

EU representative: 1st Floor, The Liffey Trust Centre,
117-126 Sheriff Street Upper, Dublin 1 D01 YC43

Library of Congress Cataloging-in-Publication Data has been applied for.

ISBN: 978-0-7534-7876-9 (Hardcover)
ISBN: 978-0-7534-7877-6 (Paperback)

Kingfisher books are available for special promotions and premiums.
For details contact: Special Markets Department, Macmillan, 120 Broadway,
New York, NY 10271

For more information, please visit www.kingfisherbooks.com

Printed in China
9 8 7 6 5 4 3 2 1
1TR/0722/WKT/RV/128MA

CONTENTS

Introduction   4

Getting Started   6

Piece Patrol   8

The Game Players   24

Grand Masters   50

Index   64

Introduction
Sissa

According to ancient myth, many, many years ago, I invented a game that some say is an ancestor of chess. I lived in India—perhaps as an adviser to a powerful king—and my game was called *chaturanga*. It used a checkered board but had a completely different set of rules from the ones that govern chess today. It also had some pretty unusual pieces, like elephants and chariots.

The first records of the game you call chess date back around 1,400 years and are written in Arabic and Persian. If it is true that this game was based on mine, it has certainly gone through a lot of changes over the years. The modern game has its roots in Spain in the 1400s and spread to other countries. The rules played now were mostly set in the 1860s, but every so often a new one is written. The last rule was added in 2014. It says the game is a draw (tie) if no piece is captured after 75 moves—*and* no pawns have moved. That sounds like a sensible idea to me. Read on if you want to know more about the game. Experts say it takes a day to learn how to play chess and a lifetime to master the game. Better get started, I say!

Getting Started
Chess Basics

A game for two players, chess is a battle of wits and cunning with a sprinkling of skill. The aim is to trap your opponent's king by using your pieces to take over the board, capturing enemy pieces as you go.

✸ To start a game, the board is set up as shown opposite.

✸ The king and queen occupy the two center squares of their rank. The queen always stands on her own color.

✸ White starts the game, after which the players take turns to move.

✸ Each piece moves in a special way (see Chapter 1).

✸ The king is the only piece that cannot be captured. If your opponent's king is under attack and cannot escape, the game is over—you win!

● Players often toss a coin to decide who plays white and starts the game
● In 2019, in a bid to raise awareness for social equality, grand masters Magnus Carlsen and Anish Giri broke the rule and started a game with black

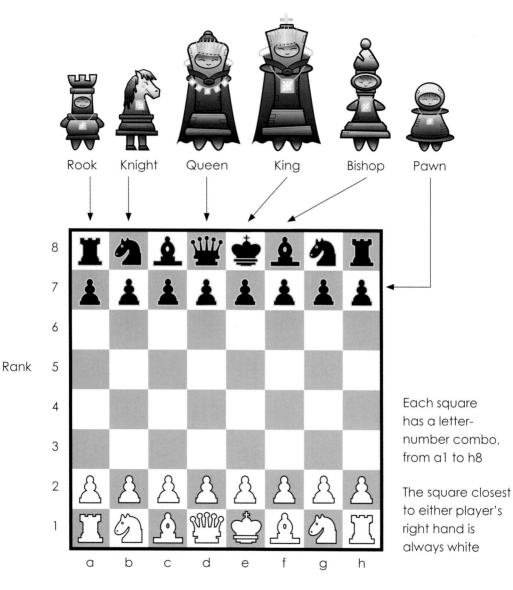

Rook Knight Queen King Bishop Pawn

Rank

8 7 6 5 4 3 2 1

a b c d e f g h

File

Each square has a letter-number combo, from a1 to h8

The square closest to either player's right hand is always white

Chapter 1
Piece Patrol

Attention! Welcome to the team, Great Leader. We are at your service and ready to move at your every command. We share one goal: to win the game. Please take some time to get to know all of us—you'll find we have a wide range of skills and everything you need to win. Learn how to use us: we often work best in little subteams that get together to attack and defend. We are your army, and you are the supreme commander. Happily, after each battle, win or lose, we are always ready to fight another day. We're ready to play. Are you?

The Board

The Pawns

Bishop

Knight

Rook

Queen

King

The Board
■ Piece Patrol

☀ This checkered chap sets the stage
☀ A square of squares, half white and half black
☀ Each square is named using a set of coordinates (a1 to h8)

Let's set it all out—I'm the solid foundation of chess, the very thing that the game is played on. Simple and squared up, I'm built from 64 smaller squares, neatly ordered in eight ranks (rows) and eight files (columns). I'm famously checkered: half my squares are light in color— I just call them white—and the other half are dark, or black.

Each member of the Piece Patrol moves in a certain way to get from one square to another, following paths set out in the rules. If one of them lands on a square occupied by a piece from the other side, the opposing piece is captured and must leave the board. Ready to play? I have one hard-and-fast rule—"white on the right": the bottom right square must always be white. Now arrange the pieces; they all have their place. It's game time!

● The oldest chess set is from Uzbekistan and is 1,300 years old
● The largest board is in Medicine Hat, Canada; each side is 19.3 ft. (5.89 m) long
● The biggest competitions have hundreds of chessboards in one playing hall

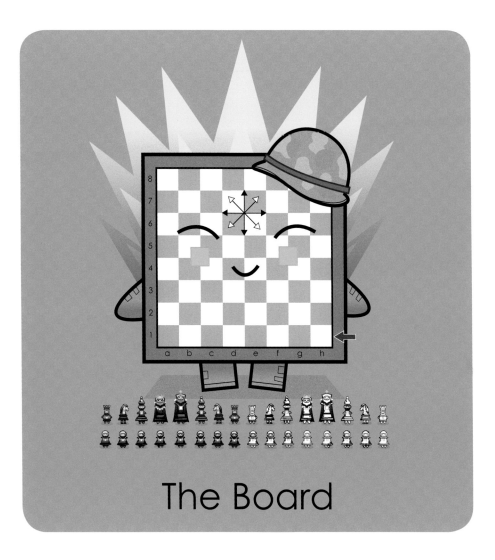

The Board

The Pawns
■ Piece Patrol

✷ Eight little troopers who make most of the early moves
✷ With no reverse, these scrappers only advance into danger
✷ Small and weak alone, together they are a powerful force

At the beginning of a game, we line up on the second and seventh ranks to form a solid wall. We are very familiar with Opening, but few of us ever get to see Endgame because Sacrifice often calls on us to protect the other, more powerful members of the Piece Patrol.

We Pawns can only move forward, never back. On our first move, we can surge ahead by two squares, but after that, we step forward one square at a time. Working together to form a chain—each defending another— we fight to control The Board's squares. If a piece of any color is directly ahead on a file, we must stay put. We take other pieces by sliding diagonally. This is when we really shine, zigzagging across The Board, attacking and defending at the same time. We stand ready.

● The word "pawn" comes from the Latin word for foot soldier
● In medieval sets, pawns each had different jobs, such as doctor or farmer
● A pawn is worth 1 point, the lowest value of any chess piece

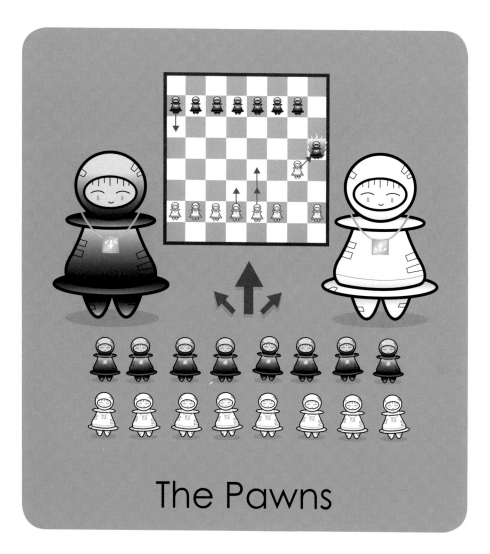

The Pawns

Bishop
■ Piece Patrol

☀ This silent assassin strikes from a distance
☀ A diagonal drifter that always sticks to one color
☀ Between two of them, they have the whole board covered

Bless you, but don't be fooled by my priestly posing. I glide between the gaps, striking swiftly. Keeping my distance for the most part, I can cross The Board in one move and slide out of trouble just as smoothly. I'm a stealthy assassin who is especially dangerous when working with others.

I can move in any direction and cross any number of squares, but I always take a diagonal path and must stay on a straight line for each go. Over the game, I'll zigzag across The Board, and you'll always find me on the same color I started the game on. Each player has two of me, one on black and the other on white. Together we can take control of The Board's diagonals, slicing our way through the game. Any enemy piece that strays across our paths had better start praying for mercy!

● In older chess sets, the bishop was an archer
● The modern piece has a curved head that looks like a miter, a bishop's hat
● A bishop is considered to have the same strength as a knight or three pawns

Bishop

Knight
■ Piece Patrol

✳ This horse-faced bruiser jumps at the chance for a fight
✳ The only piece that can leap over others
✳ Uses an L-shaped move to unleash havoc

Saddle up and get ready for a rough ride. I'm one of a pair who go in for close-quarters combat. I can gallop right into enemy territory, thanks to my special moves. Just watch as I jump over other pieces (of any color). This gets me into the game early, leaping over The Pawns during Opening and taking the fight to the enemy.

No member of the Piece Patrol can hide behind defenders; not even Castling makes King safe from me. Onward I go, but not in a straight line. No, I like to mix it up with an L-shaped leap, surging two squares forward and sliding one to the side. Unlike Rook, Bishop, and Queen, long-distance dashes are out of my reach. But swishing and slashing in any direction, my L-shaped groove creates a danger zone all around me. Let's ride!

● The knight is one of the original pieces from the earliest form of chess
● Useful early in the game, a knight seldom lasts to the end
● The knight has a maximum of eight squares to land on with each move

Knight

Rook
■ Piece Patrol

☀ Stout but strong, this tower is full of power
☀ Uses empty ranks and files to cover large distances
☀ This sturdy watchman takes time to join the fray

I start the game way out on the edge, far from the action. It takes me a while to get into a game, but once I'm rolling, I'm hard to stop. With two of me at their disposal, players are wise not to bring me in too early, because I'm often Endgame's key player.

Although I'm shown as a solid castle, I'm capable of moving fast and destroying enemy defenses. I can travel backward and forward across any number of squares. My one rule is that I stay on one rank or one file for each move—no diagonals for me! Like Bishop, I can travel far, rushing in to attack or scooting back to defend. However, unlike Bishop I am not stuck on one color and can find my way on to any of The Board's squares. Use my strength wisely and I'll power you to victory.

● Original rook pieces were charioteers
● The word "rook" means both "chariot" and "tower"
● A rook is worth the same as five pawns

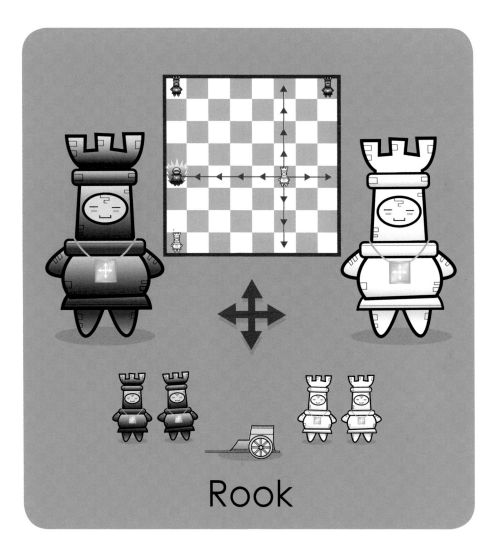

Rook

Queen
■ Piece Patrol

✹ A tall, regal character who wears a distinctive coronet
✹ A singular piece that has no twin; she is one of a kind
✹ This great warrior is more mobile than any other piece

I'm the real power player in this game, across The Board. No other piece has my strength and reach, because I can move in any direction, traveling whatever distance I need. I'm like Bishop and Rook combined. You should always keep an eye on me because I can attack from afar. You have been warned!

Starting on the back file, beside King, I like to get into a game once Opening has made its moves. When Middle Game shows up, that's my cue. My greatest strength is being able to attack and defend at the same time, zigzagging across The Board. But watch out, I'm not immune to assaults myself. Any piece, even weaklings like The Pawns, can take me down if I lose focus. If I'm captured early in the game, all is pretty much lost.

● A queen is worth the same as nine pawns
● In early versions of chess, her place was taken by the vizier, the king's adviser
● In the Scholar's Mate maneuver, the queen checkmates after just four moves

Queen

King
■ Piece Patrol

☀ Ensnaring this chief piece is the aim of the game
☀ A slow-moving monarch who needs constant protection
☀ Once this tall guy is trapped by opponents, the game is over

Help me! Save me! Aargh, I'm under attack! The game of chess simply has it in for me. The only way to win, mate, is to use Check to trap me so that I cannot escape. That's not very friendly, but luckily I have an army of chums with just one job—protecting me!

I start each game standing next to my Queen. While the other members of the Piece Patrol take on the opposition, I hang back to stay out of trouble. But I'm not a complete weakling; like Queen I can move in any direction, albeit just one square at a time. If an undefended attacker comes into my space, I'll capture it, but I need help with assaults from farther away. Only in Endgame will I come out fighting as I work with my remaining troops to finish off my opposite number—and he'll be doing the same!

● The king starts the game standing on a square of the opposite color
● When all other pieces are captured, the lone king is described as "bare"
● A king cannot be captured; if in check and unable to escape, his side loses

King

23

Chapter 2
The Game Players

So you want to be a chess player, do you? Well, we are everything you need from start to finish, plus a whole lot more in between. We're a squad of moves, ideas, and gadgets that you are likely to encounter as you play the game. Use us wisely, because we're only the first hint at what a game of chess is all about, and ultimate victory will always be up to you. Each one of us introduces so many possibilities for play that no one could ever know them all. That is what makes this game so exciting. There's always a new way to win. Ready for that challenge? Just come out to play with us; it'll be fun!

Opening

Castling

Gambit

Middle Game

Check!

Sacrifice

Fork

Pin

Zugzwang

Pawn Promotion

Chess Clock

Endgame

Checkmate

Stalemate

Speed Chess

Opening
■ The Game Players

※ A well-prepared type that gets a game started
※ Often tries to take control of the board from the start
※ White always makes the first move

You can't start without me. Every game begins with me as the members of the Piece Patrol prepare to vanquish their enemy. Usually, I work through a series of moves that most players agree are the best to follow. I have many possible versions, and each player has their favorites.

My big idea is to "develop" the pieces. That means to move them out from their starting places and into a powerful formation. The aim is to control as much of The Board's middle as possible early on. I always start with a white piece, often one of The Pawns, to open up space for Bishop to slide out. Knight is always ready to jump into the game right from the get-go. Rook and King like to stay behind, but as my phase of play draws to a close, Queen is normally out in the open, too.

● Open game (fast-moving): when both kings' pawns make the first moves
● Closed game (slow-moving): when both queens' pawns make the first moves
● Unusual names for openings include Fried Liver Attack and The Orangutan

Opening

Castling
■ The Game Players

✳ A big power move made early on in a game
✳ The rook and king link up behind a protective bunker
✳ This play can be used only once in a game

I'm a special move made by King and Rook. There can be no pieces between them, they cannot have moved already, and King cannot be in check or pass a square that is under attack. Got that? Now King moves two places toward Rook, and Rook leaps over King to sit beside him. With The Pawns in front, I've built a fortress around King, shielding him from attack.

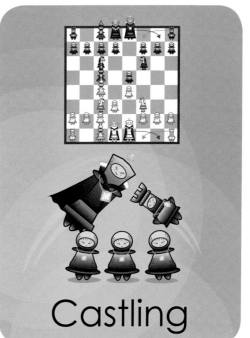

Castling

● The castling rule was introduced in the 1600s
● Castling normally happens on the king's side of the board
● The king must move first, and then the rook—not the other way around

Gambit

The Game Players ■

* This trickster appears early on in a game, posing as an error
* Gives up a piece in order to gain a stronger position
* A favorite type of opening for cunning players

Gambit

Opening does not always see pieces captured, so I like to mix things up. I let the other side take a piece—usually just a Pawn—thinking that I have made a mistake. Of course, I haven't! This little distraction allows me swiftly to turn the tables and move another member of the Piece Patrol into a stronger position. Despite losing a piece, I still come out on top in the end.

● The word "gambit" comes from an old Italian term mean "to trip up"
● The first mention of gambit in English chess tactics comes from 1656
● The above board setup shows the Queen's Gambit

Middle Game
■ The Game Players

✳ This brave battler enters a game's danger zone
✳ Plays out between the beginning and the end of the game
✳ A frantic phase where players try to seize control

Once Opening has finished its work, control of the game passes to me. I'm not going to lie, this part of the game is full of dangers for both sides, and there are always casualties.

I take stock of Piece Patrol's positions and use various moves and tactics, usually aimed at the enemy King, to try to gain the advantage. Each member of the Piece Patrol controls some space—the squares it could go to in the next move. Generally, Queen controls the most space, but every piece is important. With each move, I try to gain control over more of The Board, capturing pieces when I can. This is a good time for Rook to get busy, but I must always make sure King is not left exposed. Gradually, move by move, my aim is to weaken the opponent until it is time for Endgame to finish them off.

● The middle game is the phase when most pieces are captured
● One aim of the middle game is to end up with more pawns than the opponent
● Another strategy is to block pieces on the other side from moving forward

Middle Game

Check!

■ The Game Players

※ This aggressive type cannot be ignored
※ Always attacks the king, which must respond immediately
※ A move that weakens an opponent if used correctly

I'm the cry that goes up when King comes under attack. In the rules of chess, King may never be captured. If an opponent's piece places King under direct threat, he is in "check" and has just three options to stay in the game. They're as easy to remember as ABC.

A is for "avoid": King moves to a safer place. B is for "block": another piece moves in to block the attack. And C is for "capture": Another piece—or even King—takes the attacker. I work with Endgame to finish an opponent, but Middle Game might use me as a way of forcing the other side into a weaker position. King may never move into Check and cannot put his opposite number in check —they'd both be in check then, and that's impossible! And if there is no way out? Then that's Checkmate!

● The word "check" comes from the Persian word *shah,* meaning king
● The player giving check may say "check" out loud (play is otherwise silent)
● Double check is when a king is attacked by two pieces at once

Check!

Sacrifice

■ The Game Players

☀ Selfless but ruthless, this tactical trickster is hard to ignore
☀ Sets up a trap using a piece as bait
☀ Willing to lose a piece in return for a powerful revenge move

Sometimes a piece just has to take one for the team. I, Sacrifice, ensure that their capture is not in vain. Once the piece is gone, I reposition the troops and get something better in return. Gambit uses me in Opening, but I am an important tool throughout the game. Not even Queen is safe when I am around—only King remains spared from my brutal tactics.

Sacrifice

● In the board setup above, white's move makes a sacrifice of the queen
● White's next move would be to move the knight to g6: check!
● Black's king has to move out of check so white's knight can take black's queen

Fork

The Game Players ■

✳ Gives an attacker the option of taking at least one piece
✳ A tough tactic from which it is very hard to escape
✳ Can be carried out by any piece on the board

Fork

Look out for me—I'm a simple but impressive type. I can be used by any member of the Piece Patrol if the positioning is right. My job is to place a piece where it is attacking two members of the opposition at once. Then it's decision time—for the opponent! Who to save and who to leave to their fate? Either way, I am going to be capturing one of them!

● Absolute fork: when the king is one of the attacked pieces
● Royal fork: an attack on the king and queen at the same time
● It is possible to fork more than two pieces at once, although this is rare

Pin
■ The Game Players

※ An attacker that takes control of enemy pieces
※ This power move works by locking a piece in its place
※ A key tactic throughout the game

Pieces shake with fear when I'm in play and stay rooted to The Board—literally. In my sly move, an attacker threatens two pieces at the same time. The first piece comes under attack and risks being captured. Should it move out of the way, however, it clears the path to a second, often higher-value piece, sitting directly behind it! The first piece is "pinned" to the second piece.

In an absolute pin, the second piece is King, so the pinned piece can't move at all—to do so would put King in Check! In a regular pin, the first piece could move out of the way if it wanted to, and might do that if the second piece is not as valuable. With the attacking piece staying where it is, the opponent needs to find a way to unpin their pieces. They are no help rooted to the spot!

● Skewer: looks like a pin, but with a higher-value piece in front
● Partial pin: a defending piece can move along a row or file, but not off it
● A pinned piece is effectively useless until it is unpinned

Pin

Zugzwang
■ The Game Players

❋ This funny-sounding type can cause a lot of trouble
❋ A silent danger that forces a bad move
❋ This common tactic leaves an opponent with no choice

I go by a German name that means something like "you must move," and that pretty much says it all. When a player finds themselves in Zugzwang, they are faced with a most difficult decision. You see, there is not a single move they can make without worsening their position. What they really want to do is skip a turn, but that is never an option —not in *this* game!

Zugzwang

● The idea of Zugzwang appeared in the 1850s
● The word "Zugzwang" was first used in English in 1905
● In the board setup shown here, it is black's turn to move

Pawn Promotion

The Game Players ■

* ✴ The ultimate reward for a hardworking pawn
* ✴ Transforms a pawn into any piece of the player's choosing
* ✴ A valuable boost during the endgame

Pawn Promotion

Pity The Pawns! Most of them do not make it to Endgame . . . unless I am around to help, that is. I employ a simple process. Should one of The Pawns make it all the way to The Board's opposite side— the opponent's very back row—then I will transform that little fighter into another piece. Most often, players choose to have another Queen. Endgame is not far off after that!

* ● "Queening" is the most common form of pawn promotion
* ● Thanks to promotion, it is possible to have multiple queens in one game
* ● In the board setup above, white's promotion is unstoppable after the first move

Chess Clock
■ The Game Players

✷ This tough taskmaster keeps a game moving
✷ A mechanical referee that sets a time limit on play
✷ Sits beside the board to prevent time wasting

It's time . . . time to get serious about this game. Chess is all about thinking. As a player you need to think ahead about what moves to make and in what order. And you have to think about the moves your opponent will make in return. This all takes time, of course, but when I'm in play, thinking fast becomes part of the game.

I'm a simple machine with two clocks, each with a button. After making a move, you press the nearest button and your clock stops and your opponent's starts up. Back and forth, move after move, I count down the time. In championship matches, I give players 90 minutes to make their first 40 moves, and then 30 minutes more to end the game. If I run out of time, it's game over and you lose. Think fast, play smart.

● The first tournaments using chess clocks were held in London, England, in 1883
● In some top-level tournaments, the clock adds 2 seconds with every move
● The longest move ever timed on a chess clock was 2 hours, 20 minutes (1980)

Chess Clock

Endgame
■ The Game Players

✳ The final flurry of moves meant to bring the game to a close
✳ A phase in which only the last few pieces are left standing
✳ With many pieces captured, pawns and kings are stronger

It's my job to win, lose, or draw. There is no exact moment when I take over from Middle Game, but if you are not looking out for me, you might find your opponent makes use of me first. That's not good.

Like Opening, I'm a series of moves players use to win a game. There are many versions of me, depending on which members of Piece Patrol are left standing for the final battle. Often, it's the big hitters like Queen and Rook that work together to chase the enemy King around The Board until he is trapped by Checkmate and forced to surrender. With fewer pieces around to attack him, King also becomes a power player during my phase of the game. It is the surviving pieces that determine whether all is lost or won, and it's just a question of time.

● The easiest endgame involves a queen and a king taking on a lone king
● The longest endgame involved 517 moves (2016)
● The best players practice endgames using different pieces

Endgame

Checkmate
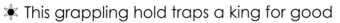
■ The Game Players

✳ This grappling hold traps a king for good
✳ A final step from which there is no escape
✳ It is a winning move that ends the game

Hey, you can call me "mate" for short, but that won't make me your pal. I'm the move that ends the game for good. There is no escaping me. I can happen at any time—even Opening has seen me—but generally I wait for Endgame to show up and finish things off.

I'm a version of Check in which King is totally trapped— he has no means of escaping from the enemy's Piece Patrol. Often Pin or Fork will keep King right where I want him. So, what next? Since King cannot be captured and removed from The Board, that's it: the game is over and we have a winner. Sometimes top players see me coming and opt to resign before I appear. To do this, they simply knock King over to signal that they don't want to play on. It's all the same to me!

● The term "checkmate" comes from the Persian for "the king is helpless"
● A bare king is a checkmate in which the opponent only has a king left
● An old rule allowed players to win by taking all the pieces except the king

Checkmate

Stalemate
■ The Game Players

✳ A dead-end type that is neither a winner nor a loser
✳ This stick-in-the-mud move ends the game in a draw
✳ Involves trapping a king, but without using check

By the time Endgame arrives, it is normally clear which side is winning. The player with the greatest advantage is working hard to get Checkmate in place, and it is only a matter of time for the enemy. Maybe they should just resign? However, while the losing team cannot win the game, they could draw if they call on my services.

I'm a situation in which King cannot move without arriving on a square that is under attack. However, the big difference with me is that he does not have to move, because he is not in check where he is. So the game grinds to a halt but no side has won or lost. I'd call that a draw. I'm not easy to achieve, because there are more ways for Checkmate to enter the fray than Stalemate. I'm often the result of a mistake. Here's hoping!

● The stalemate rule was introduced in the middle of the 1800s
● Double stalemate, trapping both kings, can never happen in an actual game
● A piece sacrificed to create a stalemate is called a "desperado"

Stalemate

Speed Chess
■ The Game Players

✳ A game flies by with this fast-moving head turner
✳ Every second counts in this mode of playing
✳ Winners must think fast and snoozers are losers

I go by many different names, but surely you have already guessed what I'm all about? That's right, I hook up with Chess Clock to get things moving along at a speedy pace. There is plenty to see here, believe me. The fast games that I create are much more entertaining to watch than slow-motion championship matches.

According to the rules, I'm any game that has less than 60 minutes on the clock, but things get really interesting if I give players less than 15 minutes to win. In "blitz" mode, I give them just three minutes, and they find themselves moving every few seconds to beat the clock. The trick is to make snap decisions without falling into a trap or making a mistake. It's fun rather than a serious test of skills . . . so hurry up now, or you'll miss out.

● The first World Blitz Chess Championship was held in 2006
● Maxime Vachier-Lagrave is the current World Blitz Chess Champion
● Bibisara Assaubayeva is the current Women's World Blitz Chess Champion

Speed Chess

Chapter 3
Grand Masters

This is where chess gets real, and everyone's invited to join in. We're the people, places, and programs that are devoted to the game of chess. That includes everything from Chess Club, which you will find just about everywhere, to Deep Blue, an awesome chess computer that beat history's best human player, Garry Kasparov. To join Garry and the rest of the Grand Masters, all you need to do is play our game. And enjoy yourself. Maybe we'll see you at the next World Chess Championship. That really would be grand!

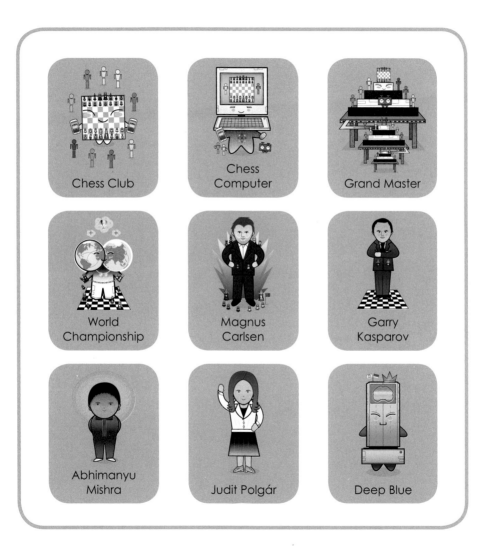

Chess Club

Chess Computer

Grand Master

World Championship

Magnus Carlsen

Garry Kasparov

Abhimanyu Mishra

Judit Polgár

Deep Blue

Chess Club
■ Grand Masters

❋ This cheery face welcomes all chess fans
❋ Brings players together for casual games and tournaments
❋ The place where chess careers begin

Welcome, welcome! Come in, sit down, and get ready to play chess with the best. I'll find an opponent at your skill level and away you go. I'm found in schools, colleges, and across the world's communities. You'll see me in parks, libraries, and, of course, on the Internet. Join my leagues and enter my tournaments—who knows, you may be the next Grand Master.

Chess Club

● The Swiss Schachgesellschaft Zürich is the world's oldest chess club (1809)
● The largest chess tournament in the world is the biennial Chess Olympiad
● Chess clubs generally offer coaching, with expert players teaching beginners

Chess Computer
Grand Masters ■

* ✳ A programmed player, set up to take on humans
* ✳ Given skills by human experts and a database of tactics
* ✳ Plays anywhere on a phone or in the home

Chess Computer

The perfect mix of The Board and the brain, I'm a chess opponent you can carry with you. I come programmed with rules and a database of openings and endgames. I can think faster than a human player, but set me to your skill level and we'll have a good match. I might be an electrified board game or a phone app. Simply turn me on and take me on!

- The Turk (1769) was a chess-playing "machine" that concealed a human player
- The first computer chess program was written in 1957
- Chess Challenger (1977) was the first chess computer available to buy

Grand Master

■ Grand Masters

☀ A top-of-the-range player with world-class skills
☀ The chess world's highest rank
☀ Qualifies for the toughest chess tournaments

Welcome to the top table. Every serious chess player has a rank, based on how many games they play and who they beat. The winners progress up the levels until they are awarded the title of Master—the best in their country. There are around 8,000 chess Masters in the world.

But we can do better than that! Next come the International Masters—nearly 4,000 of them. These heroes of the game are out there taking on the world's best in global tournaments. And me? I'm the best of the best. Called GM for short, there are just over 1,700 of us in the world. Want a game? Well, get in line! I am a professional who is paid to play, and every match counts. Maybe I'll see you at the World Chess Championship. Just keep practicing, keep playing, and keep winning.

● Grand Master has been an official title in chess since 1907
● Today's system of chess "masters" dates from 1950
● Each year around 75 people become Grand Masters

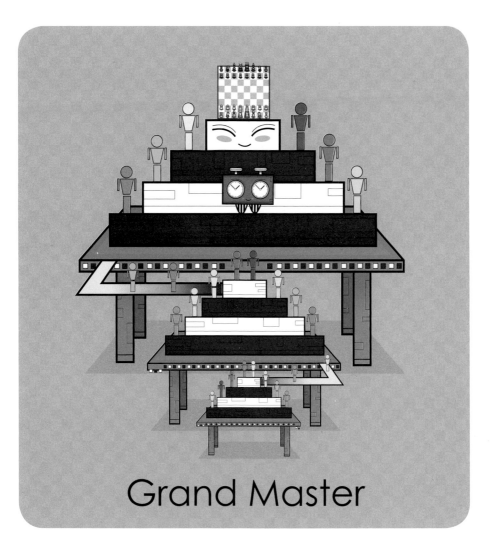

Grand Master

World Championship

■ Grand Masters

✹ A clash of chess titans that is held every two years
✹ In this 14-game match up, the winner takes all
✹ This big event is watched the world over

Who's the best? Well, it's my job to find out. I'm a tournament that takes place every two years. Matches are played all over the world to find a challenger to take on the reigning champ. The pair then sit down to fight it out over 14 games as the world watches. The winner of each game gets 1 point (and ½ for a draw). The first player to get 7½ points wins the prize!

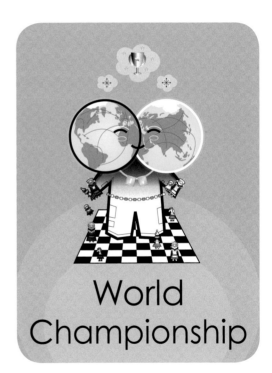

World Championship

● The championship is organized by the International Chess Federation (FIDE)
● The first world championship was held in 1886 in the United States
● There are separate championships for women, children, and chess computers

Magnus Carlsen

Grand Masters ■

✷ The number-one chess player in the world
✷ A record breaker with a long future of success ahead
✷ Unbeaten for longer than anyone else

Magnus Carlsen

A Norwegian wonder boy, I became the world's top chess player in 2010 at the age of just 19. Unless you are reading this in the future, I've been the top player ever since! I've also bagged the longest record of being unbeaten in the history of chess (125 games without a loss). Only Garry Kasparov stayed at the top of this game for longer than me . . . so far, that is.

● Born in Tønsberg, Norway, on November 30, 1990
● Magnus is the youngest-ever No. 1–ranked chess player
● He is also a five-time world champion in blitz chess

Garry Kasparov

■ Grand Masters

✷ The chess GOAT, or greatest of all time
✷ A world leader for 21 years
✷ Took on the world's best chess supercomputer

No chess player has done what I have done. I'm the best of the best—for now, at least! I hit the No. 1 spot at the age of 20, and I stayed the world's top player for the next 21 years. Beat that! It will not be easy.

I grew up in what is now Azerbaijan, where children take chess lessons at school. At the age of 10, I was already being taught by a former world champion. In 1984, I took on another great Russian player named Anatoly Karpov in one of the biggest chess matches in history. Amazingly, it ended in a draw! The following year I beat Karpov, and I did the same to all of the world's best players until 2000. One of my hardest opponents was Deep Blue, who beat me in 1997. Luckily that chess genius was a machine, not a person, so I remained as the world's top human player!

● Born in Baku, Azerbaijan, on April 13, 1963
● Won 15 pro tournaments between 1981 and 1990—a record winning streak
● In 1985, Kasparov played 15 chess computers all at once; he won every game!

Garry Kasparov

Abhimanyu Mishra

■ Grand Masters

✷ A mini Grand Master with a bright future
✷ The youngest little dude to qualify as GM
✷ Moving up the ranks, and where will he go next?

Most of the great chess players start young, but I'm in a particular hurry to be the world's best. I reached the rank of Expert at the age of 7½. Less than two years later, I was already an International Master —the youngest ever at 9 years old. And by the time I was 12¼, I was a Grand Master, the youngest person ever to reach this highest of ranks! Watch out Carlsen, here I come!

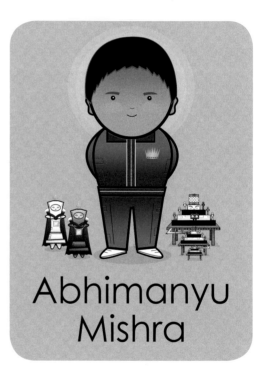

Abhimanyu Mishra

- Born in New Jersey on February 5, 2009
- To date, only 13 people under the age of 14 have qualified as Grand Masters
- Hou Yifan of China is the youngest female GM, qualifying in 2008 (age 14½)

Judit Polgár

Grand Masters

- ☀ History's topmost female chess player
- ☀ Beaten all the top players but still holding out for a world title
- ☀ Comes from a family of chess supremos

Judit Polgár

At the age of 12, I was the youngest player in history to be listed in the world's top 100 players. I made it to Grand Master at the age of 15—some say it should have been earlier. I've never won the World Championship myself, but I've beaten 11 different world champions over the years—including Kasparov and Carlsen! Chess fans say I'm the best female player ever.

- ● Born in Budapest, Hungary, on July 23, 1976
- ● Homeschooled by father László to be a top chess player
- ● Sister Susan is a Grand Master, and sister Sofia is an International Master

Deep Blue

■ Grand Masters

☀ Deep-thinking chess computer built to beat champions
☀ Holds a memory bank of many thousands of games
☀ One of the first AIs to outthink a human expert

Check this! I'm the chess champ who beat the world's best human player. I'm an expert system filled with the tricks and tactics of Grand Masters. During a game, I use my high-speed processor to search through hundreds of thousands of old games to figure out the winning moves.

In 1996, I played a six-game match against the great Garry Kasparov. I beat him outright in one game, but lost two games and drew two, so he remained top dog . . . but not for long. We faced each other for a rematch in 1997. I won by 3 to 2—no one thought I had it in me, but I had beaten the world's Grandest Master. Poor Kasparov wanted to take me on again, but IBM had already dismantled me. My work had been done!

● It took the computer company IBM 12 years to make Deep Blue
● Deep Blue's processor could make 11 billion calculations every second
● In the Kasparov matches, a draw gave each opponent a half point

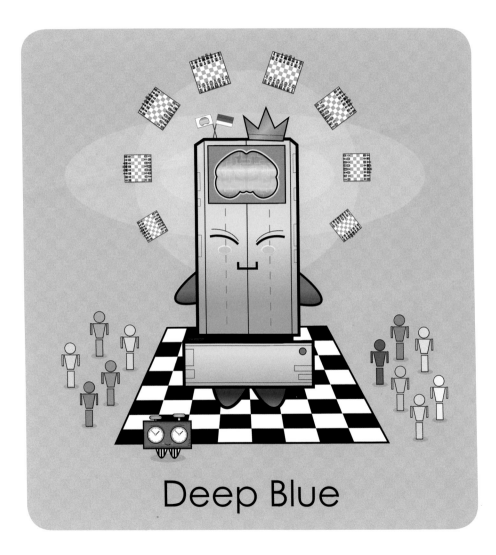

Deep Blue

Index

Main entry in **bold**

Bishop 7, **14**, 16, 20, 26
Board, The 6, **10**, 12, 14, 18, 20, 26,
  28, 29, 30, 34, 35, 36, 38, 39, 40, 42,
  44, 53

C
Carlsen, Magnus 6, **57**, 60, 61
Castling 16, **28**
Check! 22, 28, **32**, 34, 36, 44, 46
Checkmate 20, 32, 34, 42, **44**, 46
Chess Clock **40**, 48
Chess Club **52**
Chess Computer **53**, 56, 58, 62

DEF
Deep Blue 58, **62**
Endgame 12, 18, 22, 30, 32, 39,
  42, 44, 46, 53
Fork **35**, 44

G
Gambit **29**, 34
Getting Started 6
Grand Master 52, **54**, 57, 58, 60, 61,
  62

K
Kasparov, Garry 57, **58**, 61, 62
King 6, 7, 16, 20, **22**, 26, 28, 30, 32,
  34, 35, 36, 42, 44, 46
Knight 7, 14, **16**, 26

MO
Middle Game 20, **30**, 32, 42
Mishra, Abhimanyu **60**
Opening 12, 16, 20, **26**, 29, 30,
  34, 42, 44, 53

P
Pawn Promotion **39**
Pawns, The 4, 7, **12**, 14, 16, 18, 20,
  26, 28, 29, 30, 39, 42
Pin **36**, 44
Polgár, Judit **61**

QR
Queen 6, 7, 16, **20**, 22, 26, 29, 30, 34,
  35, 39, 42
Rook 7, 16, **18**, 20, 26, 28, 30, 34, 42

S
Sacrifice 12, **34**
Sissa 4
Speed Chess **48**
Stalemate **46**

W
World Championship 48, **56**, 57, 58,
  61

Z
Zugzwang **38**